K9 AND MILITARY DOGS

BY PARKER HOLMES

CANINE
ATHLETES

SportsZone

An Imprint of Abdo Publishing
abdobooks.com

abdobooks.com

Published by Abdo Publishing, a division of ABDO, PO Box 398166, Minneapolis, Minnesota 55439. Copyright © 2019 by Abdo Consulting Group, Inc. International copyrights reserved in all countries. No part of this book may be reproduced in any form without written permission from the publisher. SportsZone™ is a trademark and logo of Abdo Publishing.

Printed in the United States of America, North Mankato, Minnesota
092018
012019

THIS BOOK CONTAINS RECYCLED MATERIALS

Cover Photo: Rob Hainer/iStockphoto
Interior Photos: Mark Raycroft/Minden Pictures/Newscom, 5; Charlie Neuman/ ZumaPress/Newscom, 6; iStockphoto, 8 (top left), 8 (top right), 8 (bottom right); Shutterstock Images, 8 (bottom left); Hendrik Schmidt/picture-alliance/dpa/AP Images, 11; Romeo Gacad/AFP/Getty Images, 14; Yoon S. Byun/The Boston Globe/Getty Images, 17; Robert Alexander/Archive Photos/Getty Images, 19; Julian Stratenschulte/picture alliance/Getty Images, 21; Jim Damaske/Tampa Bay Times/AP Images, 23; Marco Di Lauro/Getty Images News/Getty Images, 25; Scott Olson/Getty Images News/Getty Images, 26; Frank Augstein/AP Images, 29

Editor: Marie Pearson
Series Designer: Craig Hinton

Library of Congress Control Number: 2018949085

Publisher's Cataloging-in-Publication Data

Names: Holmes, Parker, author.
Title: K9 and military dogs / by Parker Holmes.
Description: Minneapolis, Minnesota : Abdo Publishing, 2019 | Series: Canine athletes | Includes online resources and index.
Identifiers: ISBN 9781532117398 (lib. bdg.) | ISBN 9781641855969 (pbk) | ISBN 9781532170256 (ebook)
Subjects: LCSH: Working dogs--Juvenile literature. | Police dogs--Juvenile literature. | Dogs-- War use--Juvenile literature.
Classification: DDC 355.424--dc23

TABLE OF
CONTENTS

CHAPTER 1

DOGS ON DUTY

The police were driving after a dangerous criminal through the streets of Irvine, California, one February evening in 2018. The suspect was wanted for attempting to run over a police officer with a vehicle. Now he was driving a stolen car, running red lights, and sideswiping other vehicles. The suspect finally got out of the car and ran. The police stopped to run after him.

The suspect had an early start and was racing ahead. He was fast. But officer Luis Galeana had something even faster. He had a trained dog in his patrol car. Galeana opened the door and turned the dog loose. The dog charged after the suspect and caught up to him in a

 A police dog's speed can be helpful in capturing fleeing criminals.

Police dogs have dangerous jobs, but they are important in keeping people safe.

few seconds. The dog leaped into the air and knocked him to the ground. He bit the man and held him until police got there.

The dog was Puskas, an eight-year-old Dutch shepherd. He hit the suspect so hard that Puskas broke some teeth. But veterinarians were able to treat him, and he eventually returned to work. Officers and news reporters called Puskas a hero for his bravery.

HARD WORKERS

Dogs play an important role in law enforcement and the military. Their keen sense of smell helps police officers find drugs, weapons, and missing people. Dogs also help catch criminals by tracking and sometimes biting them. On the battlefield, soldiers use dogs to find bombs. Dogs have saved the lives of countless soldiers by sniffing out explosives.

Police officers call their dogs K9s. That is short for *canine*, which is the Latin word for a dog. Soldiers call their dogs military working dogs (MWDs). Not just any dog can work as a K9 or MWD. These dogs have to go through lots of training. They also need the right temperament.

Certain dog breeds are best for this type of work. Most police and military dogs are German shepherds, Belgian Malinois (pronounced mal-in-wah), and Dutch shepherds. Sometimes they are a mix of these breeds. These three breeds have the right combination of size, speed, aggression, and good sense of smell. They are also highly motivated to work. They are often trained for both scent detection and patrol work. Other breeds including Labrador retrievers and bloodhounds are trained to do only scent detection.

POLICE AND
MILITARY BREEDS

BELGIAN MALINOIS
HEIGHT: 22-26 INCHES (56-66 CM)
WEIGHT: 40-80 POUNDS (20-35 KG)

GERMAN SHEPHERD
HEIGHT: 22-26 INCHES (56-66 CM)
WEIGHT: 50-90 POUNDS (25-40 KG)

DUTCH SHEPHERD
HEIGHT: 21.5-24.5 INCHES (54.6-62.2 CM)
WEIGHT: 42-75 POUNDS (20-35 KG)

LABRADOR RETRIEVER
HEIGHT: 21.5-24.5 INCHES (54.6-62.2 CM)
WEIGHT: 55-80 POUNDS (25-35 KG)

WORK HISTORY

Dogs have a long history of military and police work. Several thousand years ago, large dogs were used to attack enemy soldiers on the battlefield. But their job has changed since then. From World War I (1914–1918) through the Vietnam War (1954–1975), dogs did a variety of work. They helped find hidden enemy soldiers. They guarded camps and barked if enemies approached. They even served as mascots. Today the biggest job of military dogs is bomb detection.

Dogs have also helped police for a long time. Hound dogs tracked criminals as far back as the Middle Ages (400s–1400s). Police started using dogs more often beginning in the 1800s in Europe. The dogs would walk with policemen on patrol and help protect them. Today dogs continue to help police in a variety of ways.

WAR HERO

One of the most famous war dogs of all time was a little terrier named Stubby. He started as a World War I mascot but became a hero on the battlefield. He warned soldiers of mustard gas attacks and even helped capture a German spy. The US Army awarded him the rank of honorary sergeant.

SUPER NOSES

A dog's nose is an extremely powerful tool. It is thousands of times stronger than a human nose. When a dog has the right training, its nose can be very helpful to the police and military. Scent detection is the top reason police officers and soldiers use dogs.

Dogs have approximately 300 million smell receptors in their noses. A human has approximately 6 million. In addition to having more smell receptors, a dog's nose is built to analyze smells better. Dogs can hold scents in their noses much longer than people can. Dogs are also much better at separating different odors. For example, a person walking into a kitchen might be

Police dogs may be trained to follow human trails to find missing people.

able to smell a chocolate cake baking, but that person cannot smell every ingredient in the cake separately. Dogs, however, can smell the butter, sugar, eggs, flour, and everything else individually. Dogs can also smell very diluted odors. If 1 teaspoon (4 g) of sugar is mixed into a cup of coffee, a person can taste it. But a dog can smell that 1 teaspoon (4 g) of sugar if it's mixed into two Olympic-sized swimming pools.

MILITARY BOMB SNIFFERS

In the recent wars in Iraq and Afghanistan, roadside bombs have killed or injured thousands of American soldiers. These bombs are called improvised explosive devices (IEDs). Enemies place IEDs on the ground, buried along a road or in debris. The bombs then explode when people step on them or vehicles run over them. Soldiers have a hard time seeing IEDs because they're carefully hidden. But dogs can find these bombs.

SIGHTS AND SOUNDS

A dog's ability to smell is its strongest sense. But dogs have other extraordinary senses too. Dogs have very good hearing. They can hear approximately four times better than people! They also see in the dark better than humans. All these senses help them with military and police work.

They learn to identify the chemicals and materials used to make bombs. Many militaries train dogs to sniff out IEDs and warn soldiers.

Dyngo is one of many military dogs who has helped save lives. One day in 2010, approximately 20 US soldiers were ambushed in Afghanistan. They needed to escape. But the soldiers knew the nearby roads might have bombs. They set Dyngo to work. Dyngo sniffed out two IEDs buried underground. The bombs were big enough to kill many people. Because of Dyngo, the soldiers were able to avoid the bombs and stay safe as they retreated.

Dyngo served in Afghanistan for seven months. In that time, he found 370 pounds (170 kg) of explosives and four IEDs. His work helped to save many lives. The dog's handler was Staff Sergeant Justin Kitts. A dog's handler is the person who works with the dog. The handler helps with the dog's continual training, gives it commands while working, and takes care of the dog. The military gave Kitts and Dyngo a Bronze Star Medal. That medal is awarded for heroic service.

MWDs save soldiers' lives by finding dangerous explosives.

Military dogs are also trained to track down people by smell. One day in 2011 in Afghanistan, three enemy fighters attacked a squad of US Marines. The fighters shot at the marines and then ran to a nearby village. The fighters were trying to blend in with the villagers so the marines could not find them. But the marine dog handler took Lex, his Belgian Malinois, to the spot where the men fired at them. Lex sniffed around and got the enemy's scent. Then the handler, Sergeant Mark Vierig, told Lex to find the men. The dog headed straight to the village.

Lex tracked the scent all through the village and never lost the smell. The dog led the marines straight to one of the shooters, and the marines were able to capture the man.

ENFORCING THE LAW

Like the military, police use their K9s to sniff out deadly weapons. They also use K9s to find dead bodies, missing people, illegal drugs, and other things. For example, if an officer pulls over a car and thinks the driver might be using illegal drugs, the policeman might call in a dog for help. The K9 would then search the car for hidden drugs. Dogs can find drugs even if they are very well hidden.

In 2015, law enforcement in southern California stopped two drivers at different locations. Between the two vehicles, the men had more than $1.4 million of drugs wrapped up and hidden in their gas tanks. The men thought the smell of gas would hide the drug odor. But the police K9s were still able to smell the drugs, and law enforcement arrested the men.

SCENT SCHOOL

Trainers use rewards to teach dogs to locate smells. Most detection dogs love to play with toys. A trainer will sometimes start by teaching a dog to look for a toy. That toy has been given a certain odor. When the dog finds the toy, it is rewarded by getting to play with that object. The dog begins to associate the odor with getting to play with the toy. Eventually the toy is taken away and the dog searches only for the odor. Then, when the dog finds the smell, the trainer rewards the dog with an exciting toy.

Handlers need to know when a dog has found an odor. So dogs are often taught to stop and freeze when they locate a scent. They are sometimes trained to lie down or sit next to the odor.

A trained dog does not make many mistakes with its nose. The military requires bomb detection dogs to be 95 percent accurate before they can go to work. The military spends approximately 60 days teaching dogs scent detection.

Detection dogs need to learn to work in a variety of environments.

A SHOW OF FORCE

Police departments and militaries do not use dogs only for their noses. They also use dogs for their speed and teeth. Dogs can be trained to chase after criminals, bite them, and hold on until officers make an arrest. This is called patrol work. Just seeing a police dog can be intimidating. That is part of the reason law enforcement uses dogs. Sometimes the sight of a dog is enough to make criminals give up. Nobody wants to be bitten by a dog.

Sometimes just the presence of a police or military dog can enable officers or soldiers to work without using force.

Dogs can sometimes protect police from criminals. One 2014 night in Pearlington, Mississippi, officer Todd Frazier was checking on a parked car. Suddenly three men attacked Frazier. The men were beating Frazier and cutting him with a box cutter. But Frazier had a K9 in the patrol car. As the men threatened to kill Frazier, he pushed a button on his belt buckle that opened the car door. Lucas, a Belgian Malinois, rushed out and attacked the criminals. Lucas chased them away. Frazier said Lucas probably saved his life.

Many military dogs are also trained to bite. The military does not send dogs into battle to attack. But dogs can still help protect soldiers. In 2011 in Afghanistan, Staff Sergeant John Mariana was searching for roadside bombs with his dog, Bronco. It was getting dark. Suddenly an enemy appeared 10 feet (3 m) away. The enemy was pointing an AK-47 machine gun at him. Mariana shouted

POPuLAR BREEDS

German shepherds have long been popular as MWDs and K9s. But in recent years, the Belgian Malinois has begun to gain widespread favor with the US military and police departments. Belgian Malinois are slightly smaller than German shepherds. They are often faster and more energetic. Their shorter coats keep them cooler in hot weather.

K9s and MWDs have serious jobs, but their handlers make sure the dogs have fun while working.

for Bronco to attack. Bronco leaped at the man and bit him hard in the stomach. The man fired a shot that hit the dog in the nose. The enemy then ran away. Mariana thinks Bronco saved his life that night. Bronco later recovered from his wound.

BITE TRAINING

It takes lots of practice for a dog to attack the right way. A K9 cannot just bite everything that moves. They must bite only on command. Trainers teach this skill using a dog's natural aggression and prey drive. Certain dogs have a desire to chase things, such as an animal. Some dogs do not have a strong enough prey drive or fighting instinct for K9 work. But the ones that do can be taught to chase after criminals and bite. The dog is then taught to hold on to the person until a police officer can get there. The officer then commands the dog to let go.

Trainers teach dogs to bite with the help of someone wearing a padded protective suit. These helpers pretend they are criminals. The dog is then taught to go after them. Sometimes these helpers have only a padded sleeve on their arm, and the dog will sink its teeth into that. Other times trainers will wear a full body suit for protection.

K9s and MWDs must be able to confront dangerous people and hold on to them until backup arrives.

CHAPTER 4

TOP DOGS

Dogs who work with the military and police need to be very athletic. They need to be fast enough to chase down criminals. They have to be strong enough to bite and hold someone. They need to be fit enough to walk for a long time while looking for bombs or following a scent trail. Working conditions can be difficult. Military dogs in the Middle East, for example, work in very hot temperatures. So these dogs need to be in good shape.

A dog needs training to stay in top condition. Dog handlers use exercises such as walking and running. Handlers also use equipment such as obstacle courses. An obstacle course improves a dog's fitness, agility, and skills.

MWDs and K9s need to be strong to do their jobs.

Dogs may need to work long hours in the heat. Handlers must know when to rest their dogs and let them cool off.

In an obstacle course, a dog will do things such as jump over a wall, run through a tunnel, and climb a ladder. These dogs need to be as fit as athletes for their jobs.

FUTURE WORK

Military and police dogs have been used for hundreds of years. Scientists today are working on creating technology that could one day rival a dog's nose. But so far these devices do not work nearly as well as a dog's nose. Scent detection dogs won't lose their jobs any time soon.

In fact, there has been an increase in the demand for bomb-sniffing dogs. Worldwide terrorism has created a greater interest in security. Breeders are trying to fill this demand. Many police and military dogs come from Europe. Breeders in Europe have specialized in breeding the right traits for this kind of work. So European dogs often have good temperaments for police and military work. But now Europeans are struggling to meet the growing demand. Lackland Air Force Base in Texas has begun breeding and training military dogs.

LANGUAGE SKILLS

When law enforcement buys K9s from Europe, the dogs have often learned basic obedience before they come to the United States. These dogs typically know commands in a language other than English. Police officers usually continue to command dogs in that language after they get to the United States.

IMPORTANT CONTRIBUTIONS

Police and military dogs are valuable in so many ways. They save lives by sniffing out bombs. They find illegal drugs and weapons. They find people trapped under earthquake rubble. They help capture criminals. Dogs also provide something extra that is not in their training. They provide emotional support. Dogs provide companionship. That is something that many soldiers and police officers find comforting in their stressful jobs.

Dogs have faithfully served the military and police for a long time. Some dogs have lost their lives in the line of duty. But their skills have saved the lives of countless soldiers, and they have helped police in so many ways. Dogs will continue their faithful service for a long time to come!

TIME TO RETIRE

When police and military dogs get too old to work, they usually go to live with their handlers as family pets. But sometimes handlers are not able to keep the dogs they worked with, so other people are allowed to adopt them. The military and police try to find these dogs the best homes with people who know how to meet a working dog's needs.

K9s and MWDs receive many awards for their heroism.

GLOSSARY

aggression
Angry, violent, or forceful behavior.

breed
Domestic animals that have common ancestors and physical and behavioral traits.

companionship
Friendship; a relationship between those who spend time together.

detection
The discovery of something.

marine
A member of the US Marine Corps.

mascot
An animal or something else that is believed to bring good luck or is used as a symbol to represent a group.

odor
Scent.

prey drive
The instinct to chase and catch prey.

receptors
Cells that receive a stimulus and activate a nerve to send a message to the brain.

rubble
Broken up pieces of rock, brick, and material from buildings.

suspect
A person who is thought to be guilty of doing something wrong.

temperament
The way an animal or person behaves.

veterinarian
A doctor who gives medical treatment to animals.

MORE INFORMATION

ONLINE RESOURCES

To learn more about K9 and military dogs, visit **abdobooklinks.com**. These links are routinely monitored and updated to provide the most current information available.

BOOKS

Furstinger, Nancy. *Dogs.* Minneapolis, MN: Abdo Publishing, 2014.

Hamilton, S. L. *Dogs.* Minneapolis, MN: Abdo Publishing, 2014.

Mooney, Carla. *Remarkable Military Animals.* Minneapolis, MN: Abdo Publishing, 2015.

INDEX

ABOUT THE AUTHOR

Parker Holmes has written numerous nonfiction books for children, ranging from snakes to sports. He especially likes writing books about animals. He and his family live in Daphne, Alabama.